'Expressions'

From the Inside Out

Rhoda Galgiani

A Passionately Fair Publisher
Self edited by Author / Poet
Manuscript formatting, cover designing
And interior artwork done
By
Pat Simpson
www.apfpublisher.com

ISBN: 978-1-257-87061-5

Dedication

This book of poetry is dedicated to
to my long time email buddy and fellow poet

Karen O'Leary

for without her continuous support,
upbeat personality, positive attitude and
faith in me, I may not have believe enough in
myself to continue my path of expression.

I am forever grateful to you -

Love is Life,
Life is Love
Without Either
There is No Being

Thus, a Poet was born!

Contents

Contents

Contents

Contents

Contents

Acknowledgements

'Expressions' would like to thank publisher and editor

Patricia Farnsworth-Simpson

for her generosity, faith and encouragement
in guiding me to be published with my
own book of poetry. She is a published
Author and Owner of -

The Writers and Poetry Alliance

http://www.apfpublisher.com

I also would like to thank the

Members

of the Writers and Poetry Alliance
for their encouragement and support.
For those who would like to be a part
of this writers' website, please refer to -

http://thewritersandpoetryalliance.com/

When I Think of Her

She is called Chesakat

When I think of her, what comes to mind
is gentleness, a soft sort of a person who is
sensitive to all those who are around her.

Maybe too sensitive for her own good,
she trudges along, getting swallowed up by the
harshness of the bitter souls who surround her.

Although she fights to be strong against the
evil devils of this wake again, she is consumed
by the tongues, that spit fireballs along her path.

She turns her head and continues her journey's path
knowing in her mind that her stroll will be ending, again,
the peace and loving nature she desires will come.

Through her own strength and guidance from those
who surely care, the will to carry on, too continue her
stride will conquer the hell that she must endure -

as she reaches for the footsteps in the sand.

The Lonely Whippoorwill

The cry of the lonely
Whippoorwill penetrates the soul.
His cry says, I love you.

Listen to him, hear his lonely words
Through the silence of the forest,
His cries echoing for all too hear.

Long ago I heard
The lonely Whippoorwill
And his words of everlasting love.

Now he is silent
For the Whippoorwill
Has left me
And cry's his words
I love you, to a new love.

I Am the Mother Cat

The blush of the morning dawn capture
my sleepy eyes waking to another day.
Slowly I turn, untangling myself from the
twisted sheets to see six eyes staring at this
groggy face still sleepy from the night before.

My three furry kitties, who are my family now,
Missy, Max and Mai Ling are looking at me adoringly to
see if I am going to get up or turn over to snooze again.
I slowly turn and they walk to the other side of my still
sleepy body knowing I will say, “Ok, let’s get up”.

Slowly I crawl out of bed, searching for my slippers which they have hidden from me during play time, I then wander to the kitchen making the same statement each and every morning, "Ok, let me make my coffee, first!" All three sit and patiently wait to see what I will do.

I give in again, mix their food lovingly and serve my kitties. They eat until they are full, walking away licking their chops having a comforting sense of peace amongst the three of them. Missy looks at Max and Mai Ling with a purr in her voice stating, "She's a good Mom, isn't she…our Mother Cat!"

Cleansing of the Soul

Weeping cleanses the soul,
for it washes all the stale
unwanted, misguided, misgivings,
so there is a clear window
to view the real world.

Somewhere, somehow one gets
on the wrong track and views
through their window a vision
of reality that is not truth.

Clearing the thoughts of one's mind,
a cleansing occurs, so that one
may see clearly, making choices
and going forth on one's path.

Although weary by this journey,
the effort is well worth while,
for the cleansing of the mind
gives powerful direction to -

the reality of one's own world.

This is Life

Things go wrong in a
funny sort of a way,
people say this is life,
that's what they say.

Some have it lucky
life seems to go their way,
others have to struggle,
it just isn't their day.

It's said, earth is hell
a place we're passing through.
It's home, that is preparing us
for eternity, me and you.

For all of us that are good
this hell is our learning school,
we've been put here on earth
to learn the golden rule.

Until my time comes to
go to a heavenly place,
I'll wait for God's whispers
my time is in his grace.

Season of Rebirth

The glow of sunlight embraces nature,

warming the inner soul.

The revolving of time

ensures us of a new beginning

and at the end of that season,

again we will be reborn.

As the bloom opens

to full strength, so do we.

A whisper of doubt may cause

us to weave and bend,

only to come back even stronger,

like the blossom reaching for the sun.

Life has many seasons.

As time passes, so will we,

knowing we have left our mark.

Our roots are deep,

deeper than the tree of life itself,

spreading out in many directions.

Determined are we to fulfill our destiny,

to carry out the pattern,

Knowing full well this is what shall be.

With you it will be everlasting,

for you have captured my heart

and sealed it with love.

New Dawn of Reality

A thousand mile journey completes
the destiny of thy awaited fate.
Scars upon the burning soles of thy feet
reminds the traveler of the harsh toils past.

No more, shall there be such a journey,
for the toll has been paid and the
goodness of the future is at hand.
Peace shall come to thy longing spirit.

The beginning of a new and uplifting
day has risen for thy who has
waited so patiently, for it to come.
Lessons harshly learned are forgiven.

Silent no more, thy shouts with joy

at the coming of the new dawn of reality,

happiness to start afresh is waiting thee.

Penetrating wounds have been put aside,

for thy wounds have silently healed.

Glory to thee who shall live again,

who had the strength to set forth

on the path to a new beginning for,

this wondrous world awaits you -

thy beginning has just begun to live,

as trusting in oneself radiates.

Without a Second Thought

Time is an ever-flowing adventure,
for it moves forward,
without a second thought.
As the earth revolves,
the sun rises and sets according
to the time clock of the universe.

As we awake in the morning
we know the sun will rise,
for we have always known.
Just as we know the rain,
wind and clouds will be there
on a timely basis.

Time may move slowly or swish
swiftly by, depending on who
we are or where we may be.

Sometimes it creeps ever so slowly,
we dream wishing time would speed up
to get us through our hour of woe.

Suddenly it speeds by and we
wish it would slow down again,
giving us more time to savior
our moment of peaceful serenity.

Learning long ago time
stands not a moment still,
I will use time wisely,
for time shan't wait for me.

I Know Not Why

I cry, I know not why
I feel no sadness,
no regret or shame

I cry, I know not why
this is where I wish to be,
there is no one to blame

I cry, I know not why
tears that are not real,
I shall wipe them away

I cry, I know not why
myself I shall be,
on with life, I hear myself say

I cry, I know not why
life has passed my by,
with such a whirlwind

I cry, I know not why
So little time to get ahead,
I must hurry, hurry too win

I cry, I know not why
alone, I am to be strong,
yes, I shall go on

I cry, I know not why
for I have the faith to carry,
this heavy load of woe

I Search

Hungry to frolic through the hills,
to wander through nature's beauty
ramble down life's highway,
I search.

Looking to glorious nature and
all of her mighty wonders,
to feel the burning sun and
cool, gentle breezes,
I search.

Eager to learn life's lessons,
to grasp all that there is to
see and to be in my mind,
I search.

Longing to feel fulfilled again,
the serenity and gentleness of love,
I search.

Waiting for the touch of stability,
the longing, forever to depart
I search - for me.

In Solitude

Anger swells with the growing
rage of the day by day
unrest of the one lost

Soon the unrest will
dissipate and becomes solemn
within one's own peace

For it has been taught
so harshly the tools
of the living trade

I now take my tools and
choose to craft my own life -

in solitude

Solitude's Inner Peace

Solitude brings to one an inner peace,
savored and nourished for without
this sensation embedded deep within,
a rush of volcanic eruption would ascend.

One has been granted this worthy seclusion,
for without this inner knowledge that was
born within the spirit's canvas of the body,
one would not arrive to their spiritual space.

The secret comes from deep within,
crying to come out spreading this seed
amongst the world of despair and confusion,
sharing the truth that is buried within us all.

Solitude for many may be a learning tool,
teaching those of discontent an inner peace,
giving moments to learn the real meaning of
who is wrapped in the blessing of one's self -

thus, finding truth within a stationary being.

Inner Strength

Confusion along the musty underground tunnel,
blindly fumbling, while courting walls of cold;
stumbling, falling searching to find the direction out.

Aimlessly turning towards another moist hallway to find
dark passage blocked by another forbidden obstacle;
running, feverishly to start again, only to fall to twisted fate.

Perspiration comes to the weary brow, flowing into the eyes
causing blindness as confusion of become lost grows;
shouting voices blurs the mind creates complex direction.

Sweltering heat within the soul of unrest,
burdened shoulders fall heavily in defeat;
footings will no longer carry such a heavy load.

Frail frame of oneself reaches tall to stand alert,
reaching for the sanctuary of a promised life beyond;
turning point from desperation to yearning breath waits -

the inner strength shall withstand it all - alone.

The Power of Faith

The sweltering heat from ones mind
burns the inner flesh creating holes
of deception and defeat

Crying for a cool calm to caress the
sweltering body a breath of fresh air swirls
calming and comforting the troubled mind

Peace surrounds the unraveled being
as peacefulness becomes one again
and joy returns to unite body and soul

For a moment in time a disruption began,
another moment in time the disruption is gone,
again, reminding one of progress made -

as the power of faith again, overcomes

Is My God

Love of the one I feel,
Faith of the one I believe,
Trust of the one I know is

My God who is always with me

Joy within my soul,
Happiness within my heart,
Peace within my body is

My God who is always with me

Blessings that I have received,
Truth that I have heard,
Answers that I have been given is

My God who is always with me -

thus, I am truly blessed.

Warmth to Thy Soul

Warmth to thy soul comes
but for a moment as she clings
from doorway to doorway drawing life
through the cracks from the inside out.

She wanders aimlessly through
the street of the cold damp city
searching, seeking shelter to protect
her from the cruelties of the world.

Swallowed up she continues to look
franticly for a place to warm thy soul just
for a minute longer against the injustices
that again surrounds her well being.

Wanting to stay warm forever
within thy confines of the safe walls
she once knew, she continues on
searching for the warmth that will -

cradle her soul in His arms.

My Mystery

A whisper touched my cheek
spreading warmth of a promise,
speaking a plan of what was to be

Gently circling around my tearful eyes,
opening them wide letting the promise
come in revealing the mystery of my love

Held by the arms of a power not seen,
being taught the lessons of lonely solitude
preparing for what is in store for my heart

I rise to the plan gently bestowed before me
dreaming of peaceful solitude made for two
as I come together with the one who is -

my mystery – revealed

From Deep Within

Long ago, wondering what it was all about,
I found what I was searching for,
slowly it came to me

Somehow, something was missing,
something was not taught,
not instilled inside

Others I found had this quality that I
was searching for, an inner peace coming
from deep within

Now, I speak of it often, for I have captured it
and contain the feeling that was lost to me,
I have found the secret

Love thy self, for without thy love of
one, you cannot share your love with many,
remembering -

I am first, after God

Colorless Moments

Spring, beautiful spring
my favorite spring blossoms
come to me anointing my body
with their purest of hues.

Surrounding us all spring
creates such wonders with flowers
in every glorious color blanketing
our otherwise drab world.

Think how our lives would
be without all the spring colorful
arrangements trickling gently
down the side of our creations -

a world of colorless moments
would make me cry.

Thoughts of Creativity

She holds her pen in readiness forming
the descriptive words in her mind,
carefully birthing poetry as she sees the
vision through her thoughts of creativity.

Slowly, carefully she pens words of love,
words of eternal complimentary value,
words of everlasting meaning to her for her
poetry sustains this life just a bit longer.

Poetry styles are pleasing to the eye as
she develops words of special meaning through
a clever rhyme or selected dedication that
will be read by the unexpected viewer.

Deeply feeling for her fellow poets she again
continues to write, creating lines that will
touch all who gaze upon the penned words
carefully chosen for that moment in time -

for the poet who creates words to poets,
is the most creative poet of all.

Another Day Has Begun

Cool spring breezes created from
swirling water in pools below
leaving misty cleanliness
upon ones dying spirit

Taking deep breaths savoring it all
the mind becomes gently consumed with
the beauty of a springtime moment
within the confines of the body

Overwhelming joy brought by the
comforts of colorful surroundings
fill the longing heart with love
streaming down from above

thus - another day has begun

Calla Lilies

Calla Lilies of deep purple hue,
spread their cones in glory
celebrating the birth of spring.

Soft breezes whisper through their
leaves gently waving the blossom on,
as the sun nourishes new growth.

Misty rains give them strength to
withstand another day,
to stand proudly for all to see.

Heaven guards their roots,
giving foundation to the stem
to support their loving treasure.

Fragrant the meadows,
sending your scent to all
who have patiently waited for -

your elegant beauty to rise.

Green Leaves

Green leaves of spring,
dewy mist trickles down your
tender tips falling to the floor below
nurturing new growth.

Bursting from the sun are they,
as buds come into bloom
silently spreading out to reach
the glorious sky above.

Green leaves have come again to
shelter the wondrous beauty for the
green of spring are God's fingers
protecting all of earth's wonders.

It Seems

It seems, tangled webs still
intertwine, long miles can't
break the silky threads.

The mind, grows strong
but, the web clings tightly,
tugging at the emotional bond.

The will, to grow is ever
stronger, knowing the thread
weaves around ones soul,
binding its spirits breath.

Determination, to spin the
silk into a ball of the past,
the mind sadly remembers
what it tries to forget.

Save the Beauty

Wilted leaf, I cry for you
for your innocence does not
warrant your untimely destruction.

You long to be nourished and
to grow into your full beauty,
nourish you I will for you are
the lifelines within us all.

Feed your sprawling stem
and become ever so strong,
balancing your foliage as you
cry for the food of life and
give it willingly to you, I shall.

As the cool liquid you long for,
baths your trunk, you regain the
strength needed to carry on,
to continue your reincarnation.

I truly know your worth and
my sensitivity to your needs
lead me without question because,
saving you and your beauty - saves me.

Lighting

Lighting, you come to me
swiftly out of a clear blue sky.
Your thunder roars and rumbles as
your devilish bolts dart across the sky.

Dramatically the rain comes from the black
clouds, dampening the greenery below.
Lush gardens gather your moisture
being nourished for another day.

Lighting, you come to me strikes
with force showing all who can see.
You shout your glory across the land
spreading your mighty power.

You lighting, are feared by all,
for you are God's pitchfork
striking down on those who are
deaf, those who do not obey.

Quickly running for shelter those
who fear shall turn their ways, for
God's powerful weapon shall destroy
those who refuse to hear thy voice.

Heaven's Door Opens

Rain, water that flows from Heaven's door,
washing all surfaces clean, renewing
visual purity for the hand that created the
substances we enjoy each and every day.

Rain, water that flows from Heaven's door,
a blessing rewarded to thirsty creations
longing for the nourishment, needed to complete
their circle of life, complete their growth promised.

Rain, water that flows from Heaven's door,
violent at times, combined with a light force
heard by all as the crack of the mighty thunder
startles making us shutter with fear of an unknown.

Rain, water that flows from Heaven's door,
gentle at times as it mists the wildflower on the hills, fills
the river nourishing the living creatures within her banks,
bathing the valleys bringing drink to the wildlife they house.

Rain, water that flows from Heaven's door - for me.

Our Destiny

Golden hues cast their
spell over the setting sun.
Another day has passed.
Warmth leaves the soul as the
evening breeze swirls swiftly by.

Longing to dream just a bit longer
taking in the treasures of today
casually drifting into the awaited peace
that is coming, peace that will soothe
the body and soul for another day.

Visions of today clutter the mind
bringing pleasure to the lips.
Memories have developed from
today carefully being filed along
with others of days gone by.

The heart is full with the
life that is taken for granted.
Dare do we question the events
of the daily routine that is before us?
It is said, how dare we for our destiny -

has already been chosen.

Expectations

Expectations of what is to be
does not come to be.
Disappointment of what one
expects leaves the head hanging,
the body in deep despair,
a feeling of complete defeat.

If one has expectations,
and surely feels all will
be right with the world,
one is to be disappointed,
for life and its expectations whirl
in a deliberate downhill motion.

One can't truly expect anything
now, tomorrow or in the future
because of the day by day upheaval
of the world's ways, for nothing
is scared, nor is anything to be taken
for granted, never expect a guarantee.

Honesty comes no more,
for it left so long ago, it is
something one doesn't recognize.
Truth burns the tongue
and laughter in the wrong place
labels one as a foolish silly puppet.

The learning tool is harsh
slapping the hand that it tries to nourish.
Through it all, lessons are learned -

harshly.

Reason to Love Again

Love just look at you,
fluttering and spinning
around inside my heart.
The feeling of utopia
shall never to fade away.

Love just look at you,
bringing the heart throbs,
a feeling of continuous joy
knowing everything is right,
with you and me.

Love, just look at you,
you came in to my life,
you swept me up
and turned me around.
You gave me reason to -

love again.

Love Bouquet

Adoring the beauty
and colors that I see

Bountiful spring flowers in
every color of the rainbow

Calculating the life span of
the fragrant flower's bloom

So, I may enjoy every moment
of their precious time here -

For spring flowers are
God's love bouquet to all

Word Whisperer

I will always love you -
words not uttered for my
ears to hear anymore

I will always miss you -
words not expressed
lifting confidence from my soul

I will always want you -
words not whispered as his
lips touch my neck with passion

I will always need you -
words not said with urgency
when joined becoming one

I will always adore you -
words not spoken, sadly they
diminished with the reality of love lost

for he has gone

Secret Whispers

One speaks to another
whispering secrets,
sharing words,
don't tell, I won’t.

The mind whirls rapidly
should I, shouldn’t I,
questioning, debating
holding the secret within.

One speaks to another
questioning, confirming,
is the secret safely buried
not spoken in haste?

The body quivers for
a word was spoken,
to mend, fix, restore
a sensitive mind.

One speaks to another
confession reveals the
truth for a word was
shared with another -

innocently with love.

Once Long Ago…

A quiet moment brings to mind
peaceful existence, a purity,
a cleansing, a reshaping to the shape
of the lingering statue left behind.

Once long ago… no thought
was given as to what shall be,
for it was to be, being destined with
the footsteps following the trail laid.

Moving from moment to moment
existing in a world of contentment
drifting from day to day enjoying the
beauty of it all, loving of it all.

Not concerning, never a care
nor, a mere mention of singularity
coming into the mind that was fulfilled,
that was lovingly secure, that was.

The eruption came, overpowering the
peaceful existence, the peaceful heart,
the love that sustained the body and soul,
shattered, weeping emotionally destroyed.

Torn, distorted, disarrayed, lost,
the mind wandered into emptiness, into a
oneness of tears, confusion, screaming to be
heard to deaf ears, to be made whole again.

Years of solitude giving strength, direction
purpose, a new statue of porcelain beauty,
that carries a barrier of protection forever
against pain, disillusion of untruths as the -

new body and mind conquers the world.

The Journey

Reaching out with His hand,
He touches all who are
willing to touch Him.

Follow the voice of God
He says, for He has spoken.
Heed the final warnings.

Come to Him to receive
the everlasting blessing
for eternal peace.

Do not doubt the spiritual
words spoken by the
Lord, for He is your truth.

Come to Him with love
and joy in your heart
as He comforts you -

during your journey home.

Compromising, But a Moment

Belief in oneself is a powerful
and necessary tool that we must
carry with pride and conviction.

Learning self pride, self respect
and self love is taught to one,
not born to one, not birth given.

Respect of ones soul is a need for
survival, for fitting in, for adjusting to
the atmosphere of the dim surroundings.

Defending ones beliefs and understanding to
a world that has been distorted and diminished,
to the solemn satisfaction of the questioning mind.

Compromising, but a moment with those who
wish to change questionable viewpoints to their
own mind set, to their vision as to what is reality -

brightens my own vision with truthful truths.

This is Not My Dream

Old feelings have been returning
around the bend, into the longing arena,
whispering memories of how it was,
being in love, being in a comfortable
situation of belonging with another,
feeling content and satisfaction with life.

Present structure comforted the longing,
the emptiness, the singular status
of wandering through the motions
living day by day, knowing that time has
passed by, but now time shall return into
a stronghold of what the mind is searching for.

It has been joyous, fulfilling and pleasant
as one may expect being one, being the only
mind to talk to, to communicate with on a
subject that was worth communicating about.

Learning to endure a moment of dreaming and
not being able to share that vision with another.

Trying to understand the unexpected longing,
wondering where it is coming from and why
the sudden discontentment of mind and body,
why the questioning, why it is suddenly not
acceptable going day by day, moment to moment,
why is the life that engulfs the spirit not enough, realizing -

the Princess must kiss the Frog to feel again.

My McDonald's Prince

I saw a man today,
he was handsome and about my age.
I spoke and he spoke back to me and
I felt the yearning to carry on the
conversation, just a little bit longer.

We spoke with ease, comfortable as I
felt a familiar rush being in his presence.
"Oh, I thought, could this be?
Is he finally, being brought to me?"
I smiled with happiness deep inside.

He said, "Nice talking to you",
as he paid for his coffee and
left as quickly as he came.
I paid for my Chicken McNuggets,
I left the same as I came in, too!

Nature's Loving Bond

Strong winds forcefully stinging faces
of determination entwined with
fortitude to withstand the devil of
it all that is their destiny.

A loving bond strong
the parallel between the two
picturesque statues destined to
fulfill the continuation of the gene
born between the two spirits joined.

Alas, birth peaks withstanding
the fury of nature's hand.
A chick is born to complete the
cycle as life continues its pattern
of many mysteries born to the
frozen land of the South Pole.

*Dedicated to the Plight of the Penguin

Frozen in Time

Winter winds blow the ice creating sculptures of
statues textured like crystal that attached itself to
an object that nature selected for its foundation.

As the sun peers through the iced creation a
rainbow with a million hues collect in every
crevice creating a sculpture within itself.

Adorn with love from the winds of fury
the creation continues to gather adding layer
upon layers of design for the eye to see.

Frozen in time the ice marks its birth,
visions born that is beyond human description for
simple words are not enough to describe its beauty.

Nature continues to create her wonders for all to see,
allowing each to put the captured vision into their memory
vaults to marvel again at a later date in time, for ice sculptures -

are silent mysteries known only to Mother Nature.

Chanting His Love

He calls to me gaining
my attention as my head
turn towards his direction

My eyes clearly see his vision
capturing the beauty and
surroundings where he stands

A simple phase is worded in a
gentle way bringing bonding to my
heart that will be filled with love

He calls to me repeating words
that penetrates my soul with
gentleness from his dedicated spirit

A silhouette against the light that halos
our dream like a mirage capturing the echo
of his voice penetrates deep within as the -

Whippoorwill chants me his loving song

Missy

Tears fill my eyes as I remember
pain fills my heart as I weep,
one who spent her every moment
beside me with a calm loving fashion,
is my memory of her lasting love

Those who question the heartfelt pain of an
emotional cry that comes from deep within,
can't comprehend the love shared with the
feline who looked to me with loving eyes,
voicing satisfaction with purrs of contentment

Partnership in life the human and feline
join together out of loneliness and love,
brought home from a cold shelter as it was
destined to be for the year you were born,
the soul of a loving son was called away

Time will dry my tears and the reality of your
quick departure will fade, but never be forgotten,
the pain will ease as my eyes look to the
lonely grave beyond my window sill -

as I remember Missy

Feline Heaven

I know you can
hear my sobs as
I cry human tears

Tears can’t
take the pain
away from
missing you

Trying to be strong
as I bear the
thought of
you being gone

My heart broke the
day you went away
to that better place

How selfish am I as
I cry wanting you here
instead of where you went -

to His Feline Heaven

Love from,
The Mother Cat

If I Can...

If I can stop one drop of blood
pouring from your veins
moments spent shall remain;

If I can bring joyous sounds
to your deafened ears or
comfort your thirsty throat…

then my life was lived well

*Inspired by Emily Dickinson's
'If I Can Stop One Heart From Breaking'

The Fifteenth Year

The thought of fifteen comes painfully,
as if a stab in the heart from a memory
of an unfair justice, a choice not made of me
a decision coming from a greater power,
an event that is not of my will.

Yesterday is so vivid, painfully real,
a reality that I never want to endure again
before my eyes close for the final journey when
I seek the peace and love from my God,
as He promised me from the beginning.

A single tear comes to my eye as I
remember you and then I weep for
you are no more, you I cannot touch,
you I cannot see or lovingly feel for
you were taken away for a purpose.

The memory of you is vivid as I remember
the gentleness of your eyes, the sweetness
of your smile, remembering the softness
of your voice as you whispered,
“I love you, Mom”.

I cry tears of a Mother’s emptiness,
for my Sunshine was taken that day
you saw the bright light leading
you to wherever we take our journey,
wherever is His will, whatever is His plan -

knowing we shall embrace again.

*Dedicated to My Beloved Son
John Thomas Orokos
January 5, 1962 - August 12, 1996

My Son John

He is gone and I try to write about him.
Words just don't come as I've tried.
Although the feeling are deep down inside
They cannot come out as if to say,
I am hiding so the pain will go away.

I am trying again as words come out wrong.
I miss his calls; him singing a silly song.
You are 'My Sunshine' he would sing
I would just laugh until the next call
And, then he would sing it all over again.

I use to say stop calling so much
As we have nothing to say.
Haunted by words down deep within
I pray for just one more call
To hear that silly song all over again -

from My Son John

One Heart to Another

Warm is the feeling of gratefulness,
tenderness of words expressed to one
with sadness in their receiving heart

Words are characters combined to express,
they may be chilly, unfeeling or hastily written
just because it is a thought, the right thing to do

Genuine expression penned is something that
comes from the heart, from a caring mind
spoken to one in need, at that very instant

Those who can't find gentle words of comfort of
a nurturing value, their tongues need not speak,
for the ears of one in despair need not hear

One who speaks with kindness from within,
sharing love that comes to the surface,
spoken gentle words just for a moment -

spreads love from one heart to another

A Stepping Stone

Heaven, is a state of mind
it is whispered softly in my ear
as I wander and search,
with no earthly bodily fear.

This place is there
for I feel it everywhere,
longing to go is dear to my heart
feeling peace from the very start.

A loving place to rest my head,
a place to go that is safe, tears not to shed
never again to fear in a world of unrest
for here on earth, I know this is God's test.

I am in favor for I know His teachings strong
guiding my decisions from every right and wrong,
my God truly loves me I feel that in my soul,
I believe in His Blessings that is His loving goal.

As I pen my thoughts about what I truly feel
it gives me great joy to realize what is real,
God, my Father my love for Him grows,
day to day in a world that He knows is -

a stepping stone to Heaven,
a state of mind?

Did I, Father?

Did I say thank you Father today?
I know I did, but let me say it again and again,
for the words come from my grateful heart

I know you love me Father for you show
me each and every day your blessings,
you take care of me, by loving and guiding me

I talk to you all the time for you are
my Father and I am your Daughter,
comforting me when life is full of confusion

I am never alone for you sit beside me
in my car, walk with me in the grocery store,
keep me company when I stop for lunch

My Father is with me everywhere,
every moment of every blessed day
I feel you; I know you and I love you

Without my Father I would be just an
empty spiritless body, drifting through life,
wondering what it is all about - alone

Into the Waiting Light

And, He said,
Come take my hand
and let me lead you
within the confines
of my spirit.

And, He said again,
with a whisper in his tone,
Walk beside me
for I am your truth
and salvation.

And, He said for the third time,
You are my Daughter,
I am your Father,
our family in spirit will
flourish through eternal love.

And, I said to Him,
I love you.
My faith in You
if forever lasting now
and into the waiting light.

Love, Do You…

Love, do you feel it as it
flows through the weakened
veins of lost stimulation?

Love, do you see it as it
clearly move in front of
glowing eyes of disbelief?

Love, do you want it as it
cries to open the heart letting
the emotions live again?

Love, do you believe it as it
promises to stand by your
side in honesty and truth?

Love, do you trust it as it was
carefully designed and destined
bringing your life completion -

come now and rejuvenate with joy.

Just for a Moment

(Timber Wolf ~ Endangered)

Just for a moment the wolf pauses
escaping the hunt of the hunted,
seconds of solitary comfort
a moment to recover, to breathe
a normal breath of freedom

Whisking away the movements
of nature from his brow, taking
time to clean the paws that have
traveled miles, running from man,
running from what might catch him –

Extinction

Hearing the sounds circling his head,
tempting him to move closer in their
direction, his mind wanders back
to the seconds he has as his body
feels the coolness from the ground

A moment longer his wolf heart cries,
just for a moments peace, not caring who
or what surrounds him, not concerned
as harm inches silently to his side,
not caring just for a moment as -

he continues to survive them,
as man aims once again

Kitty Rescue

My Kitty got out one frigid day
Six months old she ran away

She was gone so worried was I
calling her and looking low and high

Then one night I heard a sorrowful cry
There she was in a tree sixty feet high

The temperature was low I think twenty four
I was scared this Kitten would fall to the floor

Panic set in, what was I to do, I didn't know
I couldn't climb that tree, being old and so -

I called the Fire Department of our local town
Fifteen young men came to help my Kitty down

Quickly up the tree the young man went
Talking to her quietly she looked at him content

He grabbed her tucking her close to his chest
Bringing her down safely, knowing she was a mess

The first Kitty rescued by our town's Firemen
Lucky Kitty a feline who committed this sin

She looked at her Hero and gave a purring song
as if to say, I was scared…so what took you so long?

'Mai Ling' Rescued by the
Patchogue LI, NY Fire Department ~ 2007

Little Red Devil in Me

At times the little red devil
comes quickly out in me,
a side that you rarely will see.

Such fun during this time
quite different, not the usual me
excites my outgoing personality.

At times the little red devil
cries a simple kitties meow,
knowing I understand somehow.

Then thoughts come of who I was,
reincarnated human from a kitties world,
such silly devilish thoughts, because -

This is not real; it's just a game,
I enjoy telling my stories to make
you all laugh just the same.

My kitties are Gracie and Max,
sweet feline's yes, they are
in my heart I know that by far.

So, Mother Cat shan't play no more
for she know she's human and
has to run to the store...

to fetch lots of kitty food that
I know they will adore!!!

My Feline Buddies

Something about the feline
tugs at my heart maybe their eyes,
or their fur, maybe their precious purr

Something about a homeless cat
stirs emotion wanting to take them home;
wanting to love them so they won't roam

Something grew within my heart
I became a lover of felines they fill my heart;
bringing me joy, loving me from the very start

Something strange happened to me
a calling to care for them, to give them love,
shelter and blessings from above

and I shall - my Feline Buddies

Our Animal Friends

Loving an animal whether large or small

fills one heart whether short or tall

Without their love where would we be

no one to hold close or tenderly

When sad they give you a kiss or two

when happy they play bringing joy to you

Where would we be without their love

blessings to us from Him above…

our animal friends

Miniature Love

Spring - you came to me
a budding miniature rose bush
with a deep red hue that holds
dew drops between her petals

Summer - you came to me
your natural radiant beauty that
showered me with delicate buds
bringing me happiness for days

Autumn - you came to me
to my surprise coming one last time
a single miniature rose bud for me
to entwine with grateful joy

Winter - you came to me
snow to put you to sleep resting safely
until the following Spring and then you
will peek again through the soil -

bringing me happiness from your
structure of miniature love

An Autumn Glow

The frost and the cold of an autumn morn
comes swiftly as the lazy sun rises in the east
bringing sunlight to the barren trees

Warmth taken by the chill of the season
one gazes through leafless naked trees of grey
remembering the days of warm summer past

Pulling a scarf tightly around the neck
one feels the brisk daytime air and hurries to
complete chores wanting to rush inside again

The autumn glow lingers bringing those together
for a brief, but friendly chat as they scurry along
preparing for a holiday treat with feast knowing -

their harvest finalized the autumn glow

The Golden Harvest

Lord of the locust eating our corn
Becomes obese he should not be born

Gold of our crops the gold of our fruit
Locust singing and playing their flutes

Locust of our harvest you waste not one grain
Striping the stems so nothing grows again

Lord of the locust you seem not to care
You land on everything without despair

Oh sender of rain a rainbow cast its spell
Cleansing our furrows from the locust of hell

Bringing nourishment to our fields of corn
Protecting stalks of life and all the newborn

As life within life and blessings from thee
Protect our harvest and set our crops free

A Poet's Mirage

The movement of the free hand
glides across the page knowing
time and again moments of a
new calling will come before thee

Weary at times wanting to rest
driven to complete a memory,
a thought or feeling before it is
lost in an afternoon's frenzy

The movement of the free hand
captures forever a lasting expression
nurturing with care not to wavier the
momentum of what is real to the mind

Weary at times wanting to sleep
away the words heard within,
to sweep them under a pillow
of dreams, praying to drift into –

a poet's mirage of perfection

Sounds of Summer

Excited mother bird
flies over tree tops,
as I hold my eager cat
in the bright sunlight
of the dawning day

Rooster's from a nearby
neighbors yard crow sounding
their continuous screeching
wake up call as they announce
to all the day has just begun

Looking down into my garden
I hear sounds of little feet moving,
as tiny creatures scurry from
here to there in an attempt again,
to survive the coming days journey

Flower pedals open with a silent calm,
reaches for the warmth of the yellow sun,
displaying beauty to all who take
a moment to view their rainbow hues,
a moment too capture their fragrance as the -

sounds of summer come to claim me again

Music of the Sun

A spiral wave descends,
notes of musical rapture
dances within the wind,
creates an unclouded
moment of peace's solitude,
a moment of given grace

Eyes that glitter and shine,
as sparkles of sunlight
touch my inner mind,
flourishing
a musical fanfare,
that vigorously peaks

Entanglement
captures my body again,
twirling, spinning
me around with an
uplifting dance of
pure pleasure delight

Music of the Sun
enhanced my rhythm
as it contains me,
bringing a
sensation of joy
sensation of love -

from His promised world

Waiting for Me

One alone doesn't have the comfort
of protective arms or gentle words
consoling the human heart with
conversation or companionship

Arriving home to a dwelling that is
empty of laughter, empty of warmth
from another is lonely leaving one
to find comfort within their own self

The thought of you came to my mind as
again I went through another day lonely
and longing to feel happiness again,
to feel the warmth of another heart

I went for you, to capture your devotion
that I know was waiting for me within the
confines of your dwelling, a place you wished
to leave, a home you were longing for

Our eyes met and I knew in an instant you were
meant for me, we were to be joined as one as it was
destined, as it was meant to be the loyalty of yes,
of a human and the devotion of the feline

You captured my heart with a purring thank you,
with cuddling, sharing our warmth together as one
as it was meant to be, for you were chosen to share
my life as I dreamed together with you knowing -

I adore you…my feline friend

Get Off, You Three!

My favorite arm chair
is ‘our’ favorite place to be,
it comforts them and it comforts me

Coming in two’s, purring in quick step
one to my left, one to my right,
grabbing their spot with all their might

Happy be they my two kitty cats
for the arm of my chair is calming, no spats,
comb to the left, then to the right, tending the cats

Then one day the chair cried out loud,
‘Hey you three, you aren’t my comfy cloud,
so get off and give me some room, this noon

With that we looked at each other my cats and me,
how dare the chair speak like that to us three?
Doesn't it know it comforts us as we watch TV?

We said to the chair concerned she was hurt,
'Don't worry we won't ruffle your skirt,'
for night time is near and we shall go to bed

and then, you can have yourself back –
that is what we three said!

My Mai Ling

You came to me under stars of light
alone, cold shivering on a frosty night

Not knowing who you were or whence you came,
I knew I would love you just the same

I took you in giving you warmth from my home,
knowing you'd be safe never again shall you roam

Somehow you coming was an omen outside my door,
little did you know the love you would restore

My precious feline was taken suddenly that fast,
you came to me so my love would forever last

Now you must leave for rules have been broken,
you're healthy and your adoption has been spoken

I can't change what roads you and I must take,
but please know unwillingly you - I must forsake

As I carry you close within my breaking heart,
please remember, my love for you from the very start -

my Mai Ling

*Author's Note:
Just before Missy died, Mai Ling came to my door and lived with me for 3 years. Then Gracie was found and because I am only allowed 2 cats, I had to give Mai Ling away which broke my heart. She was the only choice because Max was 14 years old and Gracie had Asthma. She was adopted by a wonderful lady and now lives with three brothers in a three story house with lots of attention and love. rg

Memories of Joy

(A Narrative)

I view my world around me with love in my heart
for I am blessed and guided to lead a life of joy by Him,
oh, of course all is not serene all of the time with every
moment of the waking day, but life for me comes near it

I remember moments gone by a tear comes to the corner
of my aging eye not so much for sadness, but for joy in my
heart that I have precious memories to call upon whenever
needed in my moment of solitary delusion or bewilderment

Those choosing to let their moments become a vapor will be
empty later on when their incomplete lives will be ending,
nothing to call upon, nothing in their visual bank to view
and savor bringing peacefulness to their dying lost souls

Sad, the world is too busy to capture the goodness that
comes within thy spirit, sad one rushes to compete in the
task of living, seeking materialistic structures to please
what they feel needs to be pleased at that time…

Sad for them -
as I remember my memories of joy

Rhoda

A Simple Goodbye

Sweet goodbye
flowing from my lips
moving down to the fingertips
as I touch thee no more

Tender moments
of compassionate words
sweetness to the ear I have heard
moments we cared, moments we shared

Bonding love that
captured thy soul sharing
hearts lovingly whole
drift softly away for today

Searching afar
for contentment of light
reaching for stars before it is night
I leave thee with a simple…

goodbye

$$$ Gracie $$$

'Lil Gracie my million dollar Feline
had an Asthmatic attack,
rushed her to the emergency hospital,
but she didn't have to wait in line.

I didn't know what actually was wrong!
Apparently, clumping litter was the beast,
so now I use the litter that costs the least,
'Lil Gracie is doing very well but,

Mama's Vet bill was $651 dollars!
God kept me calm
so the Vet wouldn't hear me
scream or holler

something like…

OMG!

Gracie's Cradle of Love

Sickness rings from your soul
as you fill with stifling staleness
lingering, pressures your breath
calling me to nurturer you as He
brings you to a home of safety

Peace comes to thee quickly
again your strength is protected,
again your will to survive as a
special feline halo casts a glow of
triumph that cast out the evil serpents

Together we shall overcome the
foggy shadows that linger within
thy breast for it was written that
you would be given all that you
deserve, for you have been chosen

And I, chosen to fulfill His desire
bringing you to a haven of wellness,
bringing you to everlasting warmth
from His loving arms to mine as
I hold you dear in your -

cradle of love

Time is Time

Moving through a moment of time is
something never considered returned to one
for using again, for it has exceeded itself,
for it's spent, for time is time - gone

Time, but a period of which something existed,
just for a moment and then quickly moved on
to another turn of the page creating a memory,
marvelously maintained in the aging mind

Memories created during their course of time,
built with contentment of the surroundings,
the structure of life that one has been engulfed,
brings a satisfaction of the precious time used

Watching the second hand on the timepiece
of our lives, a forward movement of the hands,
spinning ever so slowly until time is time - no more,
for we have finished every minute of our time given

Whispering, I Will

He carried me for so long,
me as His baggage hanging limp,
bewildered, broken and shattered
with a spirit of broken dreams that
lived in the chilling darkness.

Crying from the depths of a doomed
dimension the body sweltering from
the heat of confusion and despair,
battling the torments of the fingers that
grab the mind planting lies and decent.

A light of brilliant glow appeared
within thy spirit warming the soul,
bringing new comfort to the beaten body,
whispering I will lift you up in glory,
I will show you the way for faith is…

the love you have been seeking.

Shore of Wailing Tears

Foamy whitecaps swirling, curling,
capturing the unknown distance
shoreline from a far off land, that seeks
reassurance from its abusive type of existence.

The sea, wrapping itself gently upon the
mystical sand dune and its seashore of wailing tears,
begging the likes of mankind to bestowed beauty upon
a battered habitat bringing a natural origin, again.

Bring forth a joining together of the salty sea air
of purity, the winds gather together the yearning
of the seashore's desire to expand into an
eternal unchanging drift of deeply white pleasure.

A moment of cleansing, a metamorphosis comes to
be within the confines of the purest of physical
change as the salty sea baptized the scorched brittle sand,
bringing a blessing to those who touch its purified grains.

You Bring Me Joy

My heart sings of You,
not of man, but of You, Jesus.

You bring me joy,
You bring me salvation.

Without You in my life
of singularity, I would be lost.

Thank you for taking care of me,
thank you for your love.

My loneliness is far easier
to bear with You by my side…

as I need not cry no more.

You're Shadow's Shadow

The evidence of a
higher power is
all around us,
as He showers His
cherished children
with glorious visuals,
glowing with a thousand
hues coming from a
rainbow after a storm.

May His tears of joy
that He sheds peering
over the vast masterpiece
of this wondrous world
He created for us all, gently
wash away every earthly,
distasteful, disorder that
has come to be within
your living soul.

As we take into our spiritual
being the cleansing breaths of
purity He so lovingly gives,
realizing and consuming
in thought that there is truth
and salvation that surrounds
the body as a halo when we open
our hearts to receive Him knowing -

You are never alone as He is always
within your shadow's shadow.

The Hollow Heart

Emptiness fills the hollow heart,
descending the love of plenty
overflowing tenderly from the
walls of the gilded spirit

Drawn away by the serpents
of unfeeling, unconcerned
windows that don't see into
a world of love around them

Life goes on as they say,
just as the willow grows
her new spring leaf,
so shall the love rejected

continues to nourish -
me

For Now…

My life is full with joy in my heart
feeling inner peace surrounding me,
knowing I am blessed

But, something is missing as I try to
sweep the feeling to a secret place,
a pocket hiding deep in my soul

Trying not to think about this empty
void, it comes, it stays, it lingers,
longer than I wish

Longing for companionship
sharing words with another,
sharing thoughts together

It is not meant to be for I have
been lead in another direction,
walking this path alone

He says, for now…
what you see shall come through Me

Golden Wings

Butterflies
circle spring flowers
that is in splendid bloom,
fluttering their wings
grasping gently the golden
cone of honey within the
center of their found treasure

Taking leisurely sips
from the golden food
that will nourish again
their weakened wings,
that will take them on
a flights journey -
where butterflies go

Golden halos
surrounds their
delicate descending
path of discovery,
protecting their wings
from danger as they
drink the golden nectar

Strength revises
vibrant delicate souls
purifying an inner core,
cleansing and preparing
for a flight ascending
to a glorious height -

as golden wings soar

Just a Little Pat

An animal's heart has no bound
Accepts all who pats their waiting crown

Walk away they hang their saddened heads
Hearts heavy as they lay on their beds

Moments go by; you bring them food to eat
They acknowledge your presence oh, so sweet

You leave again sadness begins to swell
For they want to be with you, can't you tell?

Humans and animals a delightful pair
God's doing it right to that I will swear

An animal loves all no matter who they are
Protecting them from harm guarding from a far

So, pat their waiting heads to let loyal hearts know
You are their partner as love continues to grow

Forever Tomorrow

I long for what I once knew
the love of my life who was you,
coming to me in a time of sorrow
staying with me forever tomorrow.

I long for what I once had
lost love that left my tears so sad,
quickly as special love came
it left me, no one is to blame.

I long for what I once lost
love I felt freely without cost,
secure with my heart complete
our love was tender and oh, so sweet -

My heart knows you shall not come home
years passed and I sit silently alone

Mind of Innocent's

Dream lofty dreams
and as you dream
so shall you become,
structured from your
twilight visions contained
in a peaceful sleep

Dream lofty dreams
capturing the essence
of genuine purity,
fulfilling thy being
a sustained soul wrapped
with loyalty from your heart

Dream lofty dreams
with an arrogant and
elevated suspended view,
bringing thee to thy grace
placing flowers of nature upon
thy child like brow protecting…

forever the mind of innocence's

Crazy Tiger

I once thought I was a spider,
then I realized I was a tiger

I run and growl and claw,
I yawn with a huge magnificent jaw

Tiger powerful in the woods,
controlling all the wannabe hoods

Then, I lay down to sleep,
dreaming I was a beautiful sheep

Whose wool sells for a $1.49 a pound,
on a spinning wheel making squeaky sounds...

Hmmm, what year was this???

Japanese Haiku

(Form of Poetry)

earthquake shakes thy roots
tree trunk shattered by her strength
cherry blossoms come

vine grasps lone park bench
crying as the earth opens
its lifeline weakens

weeping willow cries
wet tears sliding down her side
willow roots nourished

clouds cover heaven
shooting star has no wishes
dim vision hides truth

branches intertwine
confusion echoes within
tears ease grieving bark

dawn of a new day
wipes away the sun dried tears
renewal calls us

*Author's Note:
The Japanese Form of Poetry known as the Haiku consists of the following:3 lines, the 1st line 5 syllables, 2nd line 7 syllables and the 3rd line 5 syllables. The subject is always about Nature, typed in lowercase and never has a title. rg

Words of Poetry

(Lanterne)

Words

Stated

Creating

Love, Peace, Joy, Tears

Poems

Gestures

(Lanterne)

Hugs

Comfort

Arm in arm

Safety in pairs

Us

Bonding

(Lanterne)

Pain

Pressure

Internal

Friends help to heal

Eased

Reminder

(Lanterne)

Rose

Heaven

Scent from God

Reminds me to

Pray

*Author's Note:
The Lanterne Form of Poetry is 5 lines with a syllable count of the following: 1st line 1 syllable, 2nd line 2 syllables, 3rd line 3 syllables, 4 line 4 syllables, 5th line is 1 syllable that relates to the first word of the poem. This poetry may be written on any subject. rg

Into the Night

(Diminished Hexaverse)

Train whistle blowing
Howls into the night
Shadow covers tracks
Carries a burden
Seen only to them

Crying warm tears
Final moment
Hearing night sounds
Drowns out sorrow

Speed pushing
Train moving
Heart pounding

Too late
Lost soul

Hushed!

Parked

(Diminished Hexaverse)

My parking Angel
cast heavenly gifts
fluttering his wings
create a winds drift
with special favors

Parking Angel
planning my way
safely guiding
my soul today

My Angel's
full of love
watching me

Park my
Honda

Gee!

My Heart Believes

(Diminished Hexaverse)

Your breath whispers words
projecting love's light
shining upon thee
bringing a warm glow
to a longing heart

Promising love
joy stirs within
renewing hope
with words spoken

Trust in you
a true heart
comes to me

My love
I share

Grows!

*Author's Note:
The Diminished Hexaverse Form of Poetry consists of 5 Verses
1st Verse is 5 lines/5 syllables, 2nd Verse is 4 lines/4 syllables,
3rd Verse is 3 lines/3 syllables, 2nd Verse is 2 lines/2 syllables
ending with the final Verse of 1 line/1 syllable. rg

Heavenly Hues

(Seven by Seven)

Wildflowers of the valley

Softly waving in the breeze

Fragrant scents capturing all

Colorful hues of beauty

Misty rain showers their stems

Nourishing glorious blooms

God creates Heavenly Hues

*Author's Note:
Seven by Seven Form of Poetry consists of 7 lines with each line containing 7 syllables. rg

Moments of a Solitude Mind

(Free Verse)

Late hours, with silence all around and yet,
a stir of wind is heard blowing past the window
creating a hint of movement against its pane.

Thoughts wandering, creating, feeling, capturing
another moment in time, another moment of a memory,
another moment of an empty room, another moment…

The wind again stirs, creating its own memory,
its own mark against the pane, knowing again it
shall return another day to repeat its gesture.

Mind games play, returning to its past days,
returning to a time of fulfillment, a time of
contentment, a time of completion, a time of…

Wind stronger, racing wildly bringing attention
to her strength, shouting hear me for I am
speaking to you, I am drawing you back.

The present is here as it should be,
comforting the mind that wandered so carelessly,
longing to return to that zone, longing to…

but, knowing it cannot return.

*Author's Note:
Free Verse Form of Poetry is on any subject, rhyming or not rhyming.
It is expressions that comes from the poet's heart and mind…rg

A Poet's Soul

(Bio Form Poetry)

Rhoda

Loving, sensitive, friendly, poet

Mother of Cheryl, John and Patti

Lover of God, people and animals

Who feels compassion, pity and love

Who fears Satan, rejection and criticism

Who would like to see peace, love and humility

Resident of East Patchogue, NY

Galgiani

*Author's Note:
Bio Form of Poetry is a poem written about one self's life, personality traits and ambitions. rg

The Flow of a Pen

Rhythm and rhyme flow with style,
as words come to mind
and stay lasting for awhile

Stanza's to taunt or glow with glee
enchanting the reader
causing excitement in thee

Thoughts come to some it is said
with a movement created deep
formed in a heart moving to the head

Sharing their style with those who wait
to read their expression of feelings,
words designed by master's who create…

Poetry

Shoots Me to the Moon

It doesn't take much to make me happy
I skip along quite joyous and snappy

Seeing the beauty alone my path
Brings me happiness with a gasp

So many people can't see what I see
Or inhale the beauty deep within thee

Expressive poet and writer am I
Always able to explain to you as to why

The words within my expressive mind
Are loving and so genuinely sublime

New adventures now created just for me
'Shoots me to the Moon' with glorious glee

I send tons of thanks said from the start
Pat this comes to you from my grateful heart

*Inspired/Dedicated to Patricia Ann Farnsworth-Simpson
Author/Director of The Writers and Poetry Alliance

Karen O'Leary ~ the Poet

K indness within her heart
A lways loving from the start
R eality is her gift
E rnest is her lift
N atural she really is for…

O nly structure does she like
'L oving poetry form she delights
E ver striving for perfection
A lways headed in that direction
R ambling is not her style
Y et she is a poet all the while

*Dedicated to my email buddy and friend who has inspired me for several years. Without her continuous uplifting encouragement, my poetry book dream would not have come true. rg

Words from a Poet

Kindness in penned words,
written with grace and thoughtfulness
lifting the spirits, lifting the heart with joy.

Seeing ones life expressed with careful
selected words, one reads the open lines,
commenting how well written the pain is.

It does not take much for the broken spirit
to express eternal drama buried long ago
within a closed cover hiding the pain.

Oh Poet, release the painful past, with words
written at a pace barely allowing the pen to rest,
letting go of the remembrance of yesterday.

Close the book of days gone by.
End the final chapter and rid the mind
of the painful reminders of a lost love…

Thanking the reader of poetry
for believing in you.

Rhoda Galgiani

The Seasonal Series of Books

A.P.F.P. Charity Books

POETS WORLD-WIDE
Great Anthology Book Creators

Come Join Us
It's Free

The Stars That Entertain Us!
Tributes in Poetry by Poets World-Wide

Celebrating in Poetry The 20th Century's 100 years of Music
By Poets World-Wide

FAVORITE Poet's Poems 2010
Poets World-Wide

Practical Poetic Anthology
A Genuine Glossary of Great Poems
Poets World-Wide

'Poetic Words'
Poet's World-Wide

Favorite Poets Choice 2009

The 'Magic' of "Michael Jackson
Tributes By

'Passionate Patriotic Poems'
9/11

'Precious Prayers'
by Poets World-Wide

www.apfpublisher.com

A.P.F.P.'S Other Authors & Books

Patricia Ann Farnsworth-Simpson -
Windows of Light, Life's Carousel,
A Bundle of Muse, The Twinkles, Flick The Karate Pig,
The Wizard, the Witch and Joe the Toe, A Compilation of Tales to Thrill and Chill, Stories to Thrill and Delight,
Jack the Lad, Styles A-Plenty, Embracing Poetry with Style,
Carolyn Sconzo - My Garden is Growing
Christina R. Jussaume -
Amazing Pets & Animals, Spiritual Living Waters,
Joseph's Star of Eternal Promise,
To God Give The Glory,
Spiritual Enlightenment, Spiritual Encouragement
Cleveland Deeds Haiku & Senryu Poems for You
True life Stories & Wild-West Poems
Dee Dawn - Timeless Romance
Dena M. Ferrari - Poetry From The Hearth
Erich J. Goller -
The Trojan Horse, Groovy, My Candle Kept On Burning,
For All Our Tomorrows, Just For The PUN of It
George L. Eillison - Poetic Reminisces
Jacquelyn Sturge - Live, Love, Laugh A Lot,
Live, Love, Laugh With Me Through Poetry A to Z
J. Elwood Davis - The Blue Collar Scholar
Jennifer Lee Wilson - Fantasy and Foibles
Joanne Agee - Born To Be A Rebel
Joe Hartman - Pieces of Existence
John Henson - Shadow Dancer, Broken Wings
Joree Williams Ariella - Living With Cancer
Karen O'Leary - Whispers

A.P.F.P.'S Other Authors & Books

Katherine Stella - Time For Haiku
Kathleen Zvetkoff - Embroidered Limericks
Lou Lenhart - Life is a Gift Everlasting to Treasure
MAFLongfellow - American Pie Poetry
Mary Ann Duhart - From Out of The Pit I Cried,
Duhart Expressions Writing With Styles,
A Spiritual Breakthrough with Poetry
Michael L. Schuh - But It's Mine, Mike and Joe,
The Cross, Spiritual Thoughts on Love and Life
The Porter Family -
Poets World-Wide for the Love of Japan,
Quarter Moon Poet, Sojourners
Ralph Stott - Legends for Lunch Time
Richard W. Lamp - Ramblings of a Recovery Mind
Richard A. Rousay -
Choose The Right and Walk With Noah,
Choose The Right and Walk With Ruth,
Choose The Right and Walk With Alma
Robert Hewett Sr. - Down The Road We Came,
Thunderfoot
Roger L. Scott - Letters from the Hills, The Last Trail Ride,
The Gifts of Pendrall
Rochelle E. Fischer - Mystery In The Mist
William Garret & Rochelle Fischer - Rosewood,
Poems & Promises
Ruth Thomas - Nature's Holy Grail

*All Authors may be seen on their own web-pages at:

www.apfpublisher.com

See all about us here at

www.thewritersand poetryalliance.com

Publisher
Poet
Bard
Writers And Poetry Alliance
www.apfpublisher.com
poetryandpublishing@gmail.com

www.ingramcontent.com/pod-product-compliance
Ingram Content Group UK Ltd.
Pitfield, Milton Keynes, MK11 3LW, UK
UKHW041939190726
13854UKWH00004B/1690